To Find... Again

A Poem Anthology

Shemique Blair

To Find... Again
Copyright © 2023 by Shemique Blair
Book Cover Design by ebooklaunch.com
(http://www.ebooklaunch.com/)

All rights reserved. No part of this publication may be reproduced, distributed, or transmitted in any form or by any means, including photocopying, recording, or other electronic or mechanical methods, without the prior written permission of the author, except in the case of brief quotations embodied in critical reviews and certain other non-commercial uses permitted by copyright law.

This is a work of fiction. Names, characters, places, and incidents are a product of the author's imagination. Locales and public names are sometimes used for atmospheric purposes. Any resemblance to actual people, living or dead, or to businesses, companies, events, institutions, or locales is completely coincidental.

Tellwell Talent
www.tellwell.ca

ISBN
978-1-77941-109-9 (Hardcover)
978-1-77941-108-2 (Paperback)
978-1-77941-110-5 (eBook)

Dedicated to my family and friends, with all my love.

I am grateful to have been loved and to be loved now and to be able to love, because that liberates.

—MAYA ANGELOU

Foreword

To Find...Again, is a celebration of work honouring the author's personal experience of heartbreak and finding love, hope, and joy again! Who is this book for? Everyone! But especially for those who've gone through a heartbreak, and come out on the other side of it. These poems are of such a journey.

Today, some may experience, the often, negative stigma attached to getting a divorce, but this book can encourage, and inspire those to find love again, faith again, and trust again. The pain of a divorce is not the end all and be all. There is life thereafter, and it is worth living, and loving!

So, for those of you on this journey, get settled in, and enjoy this book of poetry. I hope that these poems inspire you, amuse you, and cause some reflection during whichever place you find yourself in your own life.

Table of Contents

Foreword v

To Find Truth…Again 1
Spilling the tea 2
The loss 4
Not today 6
Six months 7
Goodbye 8
To Find Me…Again 11
A love letter to Me 12
A lesson in humility 14
Still learning 15
Life has no pause button 16
Be like an ant 17
A question of faith 18
To Find Hope…Again 21
The Rabbit hole 22
Dating 23
I prayed 24
In the shadows 26
The start 27
Our laughter 28
To Find Love…Again 31
Healing the heart 32
The blossoming 33
Love, where did you come from? 34
The warmth of love 35
To Find the One… 37
Second chances 38

Honored to be loved 39
A Christmas Love 40
Wedding spell.. 42
Marriage is not easy.. 44

About the Author 47

To Find Truth...Again

"We all have skeletons that remind us,
We all have skeletons that haunt us..."
Shemique Blair excerpt from *Love, Marriage, Divorce &
Growth: A poem anthology.*

Spilling the tea

Sistah girl, tell me!
Is the gossip I hear,
As sweet as tea?

The vultures be whispering,
Perched on grape vines,
Tongues set a waggin'

'Did you hear about…?"
'What happened?!"

Patronizing encounters:
"Dear, that's just young people."
They say,
"What do they know of real marriage?"

Well meaning,
Facade of nosiness.
Crowds a plenty,
To see a person's downfall.

'Well, I hear the happy couple ain't so happy…'
'Really! Tell me more!'

Yes, the tea is hot and spilling,
Be careful it does not burn you!
Handle with care.
Gossip is no reckless affair.

An equal opportunity discriminator,
For one day,
It may well be your name,
Running through the press papers.

The loss

The loss of a good woman,
Is man's most unfortunate gain.
No other's fault but his own,
To throw away his good fate.

And once it dawns upon his head,
The steps he took,
Which led…
To his own error,
It is oft'n too late.

As doubt poses a question,
What have I done?
It is this realization,
That drives a cowardly attempt,
To salvage a fractured home.

The pity of it all,
Unveiled by his broken pride,
"Well, I've been thinking…
What if we gave it another go?"

Instead of apologizing,
For the crime,
Of hurting a pure love,
Tearing apart a family and,
Soiling trust with selfish lies…

A good woman sees it all,
Like a seer gazing into the crystal ball,
The relationship *as it was,*
As it is,
And *as it could have been.*

And she responds,
'No.'

Not out of hatred,
Or spite,
As disbelief and anger
clouds his eyes.

She says, 'No.'
Because her worth—
Her value as his wife,
Was never enough for him.
And would never be.

The good book advises…
"A man who findeth a wife,
findeth a good thing."

But,
Too late for him to see,
By no other hand than his own…
What *was* found,
Can be easily lost.

Not today

If it could, it would.
—Choke my very peace and,
Create turmoil from the ashes,
Of my doubt and insecurities.
But not today.
Today, my anxiety will not overcome me.
Today, it will sleep in the grip of my determination,
Until it awakens…
But **not today**.

Six months

Six months ago
I felt my spirit recede.
Swallowed up by grief and torment,
On the cusp of death,
With eyes wide open,
This mortal shell became brittle
and shallow,
I could not recognize myself.

Six months ago
My courage stumbled.
I lost the will,
To uphold the façade.
My mental state was frayed,
And with a gasp of breathe—
reality hit.

Six months ago,
I stood at the point of transition.
To metamorphose or to die.
In my mind's eye,
I turned the pages,
On the ages of my existence.

With this introspection,
A spark of rebellion lit,
Deep in the pit of a broken cry.

Six months ago,
I chose **life**.

Goodbye

I took your power away.
You no longer have a way,
To hurt me.
The pain you seek to project,
Reflects.
Boomerang.

Now, I laugh at your ploy,
Comedic in nature.
I see your colours have dimmed—
An epic satire.

You used to be the Earth in my orbit,
But you're a cold Neptune,
And hindsight is the clearest vision:
I am the Sun,
My fate is tied to the moon.

In the deepest flame,
I burn true,
And every day without you—
Is anew.

Your reach is lost,
You had your day.
Like the thunder,
You raged…you stormed…
And I am so glad,
The rain is gone.

To Find Me...Again

"I let go, to allow room for new growth..."
Shemique Blair excerpt from *Love, Marriage, Divorce & Growth: A poem anthology.*

A love letter to Me

Dear Me,
You have done it.
You have done the thing you thought impossible.
At one point, you thought to give in,
And become conjoined with the particles of dust,
But, instead,
You have spread wings to unimaginable heights,
And soared even beyond your own hindsight.

It did not kill you.
Maimed you—temporarily,
Scarred you—yes,
But you survived.
And in your own way, prevailed,
Against the odds.

A beaten heart renewed,
In the dawn of a new wake.
You take on the day,
And allow both the pain of love lost,
And the pangs of rebirth,
To burrow deep and with reverence, arise again.

Yes, you have done it.
You have done the thing you thought impossible.
At one point, you thought to give in,
And become conjoined with the particles of dust,
But instead,
You have unseated defeat,
And named *hope* your namesake.

A lesson in humility

Crushed but not defeated,
The process of growth,
Painful—
A lesson in humility.

But overcoming one challenge,
Simply prepares you for the next,
Life is a series of obstacles,

From the minuscule solving of
A kitchen problem:
"The handle of the can opener broke, is there another?"
To those life altering transitions:
Navigating through a divorce and a broken heart.

Life is one big jumble of challenges,
And even when,
We've found a semblance of routine,
Or a moment's peace,

The next obstacle is never too far behind,
To test our patience, or faith, or kindness.
The key is to keep moving forward.

And at each obstacle,
Learn from the opportunity,
Whether a failure or success:
It is *okay* to be crushed,
But be never defeated.

Still learning

I am learning, still.
Accepting the things, I cannot change.
Taking accountability,
No more blame games.

Letting go of our faults.
Mine for trusting you to be,
More than you are.
And I, for expecting the least.

Red flags don't change colours,
They blend in,
And remain,
Like a chameleon in a new environment.

I should've known you'd be,
Exactly who you showed you'd be.
In hindsight, I was too naïve.

Alas, I am still learning.
Accepting the things, I cannot change.
And moving forward from past mistakes.

Life has no pause button

Life has no pause button.
No time to redo,
Rethink,
Rewind.

Life is a constant barrage of opportunities,
A whirlwind of decisions and choices,
Mistakes and mishaps,
Discoveries and experiences.

Life is purpose driven.
Everyday a new challenge,
A new lesson,
A strict taskmaster to a,
Knowledge deprived student.

Life is at its end, but a sum.
A journey of the combined total of,
Memories and recollections,
Lived in between the exhale of,
Every sigh, cry, and sound.

Life is a beautiful mosaic of moments.
From the first breathe of a newborn child,
To the last at their end.
To start again, in the cycle of time,
Life is endless.

Be like an ant

"Be like an ant," my mother said.
Never passing a fellow,
Without lending a hand,
A helpful sport,
A supportive chap.

"Be like an ant," my mother encouraged.
Focused on community building,
One step at a time in,
Harmonious cohesion,
A river flowing in,
The same direction.

"Be like an ant!" my mother scolded.
"—Not like the termite!"
Tearing down the foundation,
From underneath.
To lose each generation,
Bloodline, ancestry, and story…
In the decay of pillars:
The lust of our own greed.

So, be like an ant.
I am reminded.
Be like an ant.
Building the foundation.
Block by block,
Step by step.

A question of faith

Looking out across the bay
I wonder at the majesty of the creator and its creation.
I, a mere speck in comparison to the might of the ocean,
It's dark waves carelessly billow with no land or mammal in sight.

What is over yonder? I ponder.
For the distance is as far as one can see,
but the imagination can go so much more beyond that,
Like *The Little Mermaid Under the Sea*...

As vast as the stark ocean and its turbulent seas,
The human spirit can be as fierce,
Refusing to settle for simply good enough—
Continuing to strive for more, for greater, for better...
Stretching its own capacity,
Revealing the unknown to be more than a mystery.

Faith is the courage to step out into the unknown,
It requires super Herculean strength,
Perhaps, it is *faith* which holds our backbone?
To depend on a power greater than our own,
To accept in humility that things are not always,
In our control.

To Find Hope...Again

"After letting go, I am free to wonder — to dream..."
Shemique Blair excerpt from *Love, Marriage, Divorce & Growth: A poem anthology.*

The Rabbit hole

Should I travel once more down the rabbit hole?
To what end or to what aim?
Is it worth the risk? Will I find a new kind of wonder?
Can love exist without pain?

Should I travel once more down the rabbit hole?
But what would I attain?
Will I find my prince charming or the love of my life?
Can I withstand the uprising of change?

Down, down the rabbit hole I go,
Afraid and alone.
Having nothing to lose…
But, perhaps, more to gain.

Dating

Online profile?

Check.

An attractive photo?

Uploaded.

Swipe, swipe,
Left.

Swipe, swipe,
Right.

Open chat box,

New message?

Open.

Hello, how are you?
I see we have some things in common,
And I would like to get to know you…

Typing…pause
…typing.

I prayed

I prayed for a sign.
Gazing out at the backyard ready for children,
To run around in.
I could hear the faint echo of childish,
games and laughter.

I prayed for my heart to be open.
Not bitter from the past mistakes but,
Humbled to love once more.

I prayed for a future.
Far from the dark sunken drift,
I'd found myself in,
And console myself with patience.

I whispered,
"Lord, please send me the one,
To accept and love all of me.
Please send me a love unconditional,
A mirror of you for your creation."

I prayed and waited.

In the shadows

In the shadows of loss,
Hope blossomed to the confession of love.
In warm arms of comfort—
A source of peace.

Love nestled,
And once again…
The fragile,
The tentative,
Becomes possible.

Though beaten and displaced, love never dissipates.
Marred by scars of pain,
And deceit,
It rises once more,
Like a rose amidst concrete.

The start

It started with a *bang*,
Literally.
Our first conversation,
A teasing flirtation,
Which led to another and another…

Memorable encounters,
Laid the groundwork for more.
A relationship that could last
A lifetime.

Our connection
Ignited the rest of our lives.
Melding together,
Two halves of a whole.

Our laughter

Our laughter is medicine.
A balm to this weary heart.
Soothing and righteous.
Oh, how we laugh—
Like a baby's first sound
To its own ears,
Ringing free and contagious.

Enticing others to join in,
Cooing,
With silly expressions,
We laugh at ourselves,
Not taking the other too seriously—
Selflessly delighting in each other's company.

We laugh,
To the delight of our own stars.
Your quick wit—
My sharp humour.
Boisterously,
Our bellies shake,
Our shoulders tremble,
Our jaws ache.

The *joy* is in our chuckles,
Our grins,
Our eyes twinkling,
Saying, "Laugh with me, my love."

To Find Love...Again

"Love steady when seasons change and uncertainty reigns..."
Shemique Blair excerpt from *Love, Marriage, Divorce & Growth: A poem anthology.*

Healing the heart

She asked me,
"How do you mend a broken heart?
How do you find love once more?"

I turned my gaze to the trees,
With their branches covered in morning dew.
Their leaves glistening,
Each drop holding the resplendent
Glow of their surroundings.

My ears sought the humming of the birds,
As they danced in the breeze and flew,
Hopping delicately from stem to stem,
Limb to limb,
From nest to field in their banter and play.

Finally, I said,
"It is not for us to find love,
But for us to be as open to it as a leaf unfolds,
To the sustenance of a drop of water.

Love is like the heartbeat of flapping wings,
Allowing us to take flight,
To soaring heights never trespassed before.

Love surrounds us,
Is all around us.
We often wade by it,
But faith is the compass."

The blossoming

Like the unfurling of soft rose petals
Or as the underside of dove wings
My love for you reveals,
The inner vulnerabilities of my tenderness.

I am yours. Handle with care.

Cradle my heart as if it were your own,
Each precious beat a lifeline that keeps you alive.
Embrace my being as if it were your own,
Value each breathe,
As a count towards your own timeline.

Be on guard, tending gently to my spirit and mind—
They too need your kindness.
I am open to you,
Lay me down in the love of your care,
And never doubt.

Love, where did you come from?

In broken bewilderment he asked me,
'Where did you come from?'
I replied with a simple answer:
'My parents gave birth to me.'
And kissed his lips.

It was in his broken tone that I found my place of belonging,
His question mirrored the craving of one left too long alone,
With a hunger so great it made a hardened heart ache,
For the peace and comfort of loving arms,
And a genuine embrace.

"Love, where did you come from?"
Oh, to be so afraid of finding the precious,
We question its sincerity.
For *true* love found is like a tender rose petal,
To be treasured oh so delicately.
Cradled between the folds of aged pages,
To preserve *true love's memory…*

The warmth of love

The feeling of love known
Is like non other—
Tender like a cozy wood burning fire,
Its tinder loving care is a warmth,
That settles deep into the bones,
To the very marrow.

The warmth of love known
Cradles the soul against any harm,
Or disappointment, and sorrow.
It burns brightly against the shadows,
Secured to its bounty of,
The loved, and loving hold between
Hearts as pure as gold.

To Find the One…

"A new connection…a pleasantly teasing sensation…"
Shemique Blair excerpt from *Love, Marriage, Divorce & Growth: A poem anthology*

Second chances

Second chances don't come by here often,
Second chances are few, and far in between.
For some folks, it takes a while,
For others the risk is never seen.

But I am grateful.
For if life has taught me anything,
It's to never take for granted a second opportunity.
When fate has called you once and reckons to, once more.
Like an eager child—run on!
And don't question the open door…

Square your shoulders,
Gird your loins with courage,
Be a sport and take the dare!
Squander not the minute nor the hour.
A second chance is fleeting,
A second chance is rare.

Second chances don't come by here often,
Second chances are few, and far in between.
For some folks it takes a while,
For others, the risk is never seen.

Honored to be loved

My God! I've never known a love like you.
Laying in each other's arms,
Enjoying the simple comfort of,
A trusting and safe embrace.
Makes my heart race.

Hearing you utter, "I love you."
The ring of purity in your tone,
Provides assurance I'd before never known.
My heart sings at the sound of your truth,
Reaffirming my faith in you.

Thought I was dreaming but,
A lucid production becomes reality.
How could I even question your sincerity?
You've never shown otherwise.
Your actions true —a far cry from past miscues.

You're a generous and beautiful mountain of a man.
Lifting me to heights I have never viewed!
Not a pedestal but a gentle elevation of,
Mutual respect and admiration.
I am honored to be loved by you.

To see where I've come from…
To this place where I am,
With you right here, right now.
Only destiny could orchestrate a love like this.
Together, we are uniquely, unequivocally, *perfect*.

A Christmas Love

Wrapped in the reverence of a starry night.
We remember the tale of hope,
So long ago,
A child divine was born to save mankind.

A blanket of snowflakes tickles the air.
Drifting gently across our smiling faces.
Strolling gaily along the glassy streets.
We hear the chime of joy and laughter in all places.

A time of cheer like no other.
Showing kindness can lift spirits high,
The allure of forgiveness and compassion abounds,
As the whole world celebrates that holy night.

The angels sing gloriously above:
Peace and goodwill to all!
With hearts open and hands held tight,
Arm in arm, glove to glove,
We embrace the true gift,
Of a Christmas love.

Wedding spell

Wedding jitters? Far from it.
Been long time comin'—
This kinda happiness.

I'm gonna meet him at the altar,
In the morning.
Wearing a white dress—
'Cause that's my prerogative!

Before God and witnesses:
Sealed, tied, and knotted.
A love commitment,
A sacred promise.

More than a marriage.
Saying yes to my man—
I'll even shout it!
'Cause second chances don't come 'round too often.

This time - I've no interest,
To squander it.
As God as my witness,
Let this be,
A blessed union,
Between *I* and *He*.

Marriage is not easy

Make no mistake —marriage is not easy.
It is a commitment,
A responsibility,
To you and your partner.

Daily choosing to be present,
Choosing to build a life,
Choosing to build each other.

When the freshness of youth fades,
And our days blend into each other,
Can our love stand the test of time?
Can our marriage last forever?

We talked today and that made me glad.
We communicated openly, frankly, and honestly,
About our goals, our dreams, and desires.
It was a lot,
And all I could have hoped for.
It was the beginning of reconnecting and recovery.

The seeds are sown, the roots have been tended.
And day by day,
Our marriage is thriving,
And day by day,
Our relationship is growing.

Marriage is not easy—make no mistake.
Love alone will loosen its sails but

Anchored to trust, forgiveness, and grace—
A marriage won't fail.

Yes, marriage is not easy but
It is a commitment worth making.
The thrill of a lifetime,
And a story worth living.

About the Author

Shemique Blair is a Canadian-Jamaican educator, writer, dreamer and singing enthusiast. She is the author of Love, Marriage, Divorce & Growth: A poem anthology. Living in the northern regions of Ontario, Canada, with her indulgent cat and her loving husband. As an educator, she works to make a difference in the lives of those she encounters. She is an avid reader who still believes in true love and romance.

What's next?

Thank you for purchasing a copy of my poetry book, *To Find...Again*. I hope you enjoyed the journey! If you haven't read my first book, *Love, Marriage, Divorce and Growth: A Poem Anthology*. Be sure to get your copy today!

Please feel free to leave a review of my books on www.goodreads.com/shemiqueblair.

See you on the next journey!

 @blairshemique

 www.sblairwritings.com

www.ingramcontent.com/pod-product-compliance
Lightning Source LLC
LaVergne TN
LVHW011859060526
838200LV00054B/4421